Little Black Book

poems by

Chad Frame

Finishing Line Press
Georgetown, Kentucky

Little Black Book

Publisher: Leah Huete de Maines
Editor: Christen Kincaid
Cover Art and Design: Chad Frame
Author Photo: Chad Frame

Order online: www.finishinglinepress.com
           also available on amazon.com

Author inquiries and mail orders:
Finishing Line Press
P. O. Box 1626
Georgetown, Kentucky 40324
U. S. A.

Table of Contents

For Catullus—long dead in the flesh, but always alive on the page.

Dear Mark Doty

Am I doing it right? I know we all walk
our own path through the snarl of brambles
in this forest, that what we sacrifice
is different—so is what we achieve.

Should I be sorry I have not—yet—lost
what you have lost, that I have fewer miles
of path behind me, that my achievements
are modest at best? That I prefer cats?

I know you will answer not to compare
apples and oranges, two different fruits
in two different lives—but maybe kindred,
I dare to hope, savored by the same mouths.

Perhaps the same lips purse for us, reading
our disparate poems, as if to kiss
their authors, perhaps the tongues, those same silk
sleeves, wrap around our words, pink and pining.

Please, Mark, tell me I will grow to be wise
and loved, that I will leave a legacy
of epiphanies and dog-eared pages
behind me, somewhere in both of our wakes.

Christopher

What the hell, you ask,
flush and flustered, spitting
the worst words you know,

the hell of the schoolbus
lurching to a stop
on my street, the red

flashing lights we pretend
are lasers firing
from our yellow tank,

the hell of the quiet
between whatever
third grade boys chatter

on their ride home, sitting
together, *the hell*
of my leaning in

for a sudden peck
against your pink lips,
an impulse I can't

resist or explain,
the hell I'm going
to be living in

for years before
I can even begin
to answer that question.

Pot v. Pan

The courtroom artist has depicted them
with as much dignity as possible,

one fresh from its notched groove in the washer,
the other food-flecked, dug out of the sink,

both clutched in the fists of the young witness,
cowlick-coiffed, in red-footed pajamas,

now too big to crawl in the cabinet,
dashing for something to dash together

to drown out flying *deadbeats* and *bitches*
devolved from the arguments on both sides

into hurling laundry and cheap dishes
shattered in the next room—mother, father.

The clangor of the closing argument,
dissonant cymbals, hollow timpani,

a refrain of *you worthless piece of shit,*
a desperate Calphalon countersong,

is hushed by the bang of the oak gavel,
a slammed front door, a wan slice of cheesecake

on the counter, unsmothered by cherry,
unpunctured by fork or tooth—still guilty.

Jesse

We were always together, once,
the poor boy whose house you'd never visit—
It's too tiny and smells like cigarettes.

Lithe. Nut-brown hair in your cunning eyes.
Wrestling on the basement rug, you pinned me.
Poor boy. You must have thought you were strong.

I looked you up yesterday. Salt Lake.
Red-haired, red-lipped wife and sandy-haired son,
motorcycle you ride through the mountains.

Do they know how strong you really are?
Do they know what happened to the blond boy
from the smoke-choked house across town?

I'll tell them. I am what the wind takes
when it blows, bits of me pinned and carried
to the bristlecones waiting on your street.

Dungeons &

two eighth grade outcasts & a lunch table
& telling jokes & brandishing a Cheeto
like a wizened staff to cheer you up
when that girl from Algebra & you don't work out
& I shout *Gandalf the Orange!* & you snort Pepsi
like flames & your cheeks dimple & you shake
sleek hair from your brown eyes & we toss dice
& I can't admit it's not an elf
& not a wizard I'm pretending to be
& I love you & I'm sorry & for me
it's never been a game about dragons.

Nine-Year-Old Suicide in Reverse

for Jamel Myles

A candle unsnuffs, its smoke drawn back in,
its guttering, finger width flame relit.
The bright blue JanSport rises from the floor
and hooks its straps around your slight shoulders.

You dart backwards down the carpeted stairs.
The door unslams. The yellow bus backs up
around the cul-de-sac. Your eyes unclench.
The children suck words back away from you.

High-fletched *F*, its bulbless semiquaver.
Lofty *A*, its slopes unassailable.
Selfsame, cliquish *GG*, backs turned to shun.
Surprised *O*, rolling, caught up in all this.
And *T*, the final, burning cross of it.

That morning, unknowing, your mother smiles,
untousles your hair like wind smoothing grass,
and sits. Inky clouds of coffee billow
past her pursed lips like possessing spirits.

Andrea

Eighth grade class photo—blonde bangs,
Slavic chin, glossed lips pursed to pout

over blue eddies of smeared thumbprints,
white dress wings draped on slight shoulders,

a caricature of ingénue.
All the boys in the gifted class brag,

use their IQs to describe in detail
all they'll do when they get you alone.

Alone in my room, just me and the two—
by-three wallet of you, attempting

over and over, my hands desperate,
my efforts futile, your wide eyes

unblinking, as if desire is a puzzle
that can simply be hammered to fit

together with an audible *click*.
You are human before set piece,

human after. One day in Algebra,
we learn the transitive property,

where if all boys like you, and I am a boy—
but I am staring intently at the back

of the boy's head in front of me, his hair
in a single curl on the nape of his neck,

how I want to twist my finger in it,
how much I need to pay attention

to this lesson, the one I will need
every day for the rest of my life.

Jesus

Everyone tells me you love me—
at fourteen, I am unworthy,

pumping myself furiously
to the image of you hanging

with your soft face and hard stomach
rippling like wisps of cirrus cloud,

atmosphere-blue eyes, parted pink lips,
tawny hair on your slight shoulders.

Desperately seeking answers
in the folds of your sackcloth shorts,

I achieve enlightenment,
everything making sense for one

brief instant—then limp and lifeless,
with only the promise that I

will rise again.

Shepard

for Matthew Shepard

There on the hill—
a scarecrow—no—

a boy, tear-tracks
through blood and grime,

slumped, arms raised, tied
to a buck rail,

and left to watch
over his flock.

When I learn this,
I'm just fifteen,

a sophomore,
thinking maybe

I could just tell
someone, a friend,

what I'm feeling,
grow bold enough

to act on it.
What is a kiss?

the cold pistol
our attraction

has whipped us with.
Matthew, I wish

I could show you
what you've achieved—

a boy, tear-tracks
through blood and grime.

Bruce

Outside, it's scarcely my sixteenth
winter, pacing the drive, unsure
what's led here—hours of typing,
the heyday of dialup chatrooms,

a torso photo, a phone call
to calm my jangling nerves—me out
the door, you on your way to pick
me up. Only the sparse, dead trees,

thinning hair on the hilltop's scalp,
are watching when your car rattles
to a stop, your cracked face an old
catcher's mitt slowly catching fire

within, spewing cigarette smoke.
Terrified, more of backing out
than anything, I creak the door
open and climb inside. We go.

Later that night, I am retching
in the bathroom when my mother
comes home from work. I do not tell
anyone there are parts of me

that will never shake free, never
be grown out of or eased into,
will never be the same again,
because they do not come from me.

This day I've learned to swallow more
than you, more than pride or cola
straight from the two-liter bottle
to cleanse the taste—the hardest thing

to swallow is the idea
that there will be no second chance

at a first time. Persephone,
trapped in winter, aching for spring,

must realize because she swallows
her captor's seed she can never
feel the sun, her mother's plain face
bearing the promise of flowers.

Invisible Handkerchief

Left Pocket

I walk into the room, saying nothing,
drop to my knees on the floor before you,
and reach for your pants, awkwardly fumbling
for the antique World War Two pocket watch
your grandfather left you, pop it open,
and twist the dial, winding back two hours
we would have spent having rough, nameless sex.
I can never adjust to the new time.
I will miss important work meetings, films
about puffy-faced Jennifer Lawrence
saving people, in the process saving
herself, and perhaps in the dark theater
I could have steepled my fingers sweetly
with yours if we weren't now worlds apart.

Right Pocket

I step sideways into my other life,
see us lying there, twined like dead ivy
on a cold wall, no room for pillow talk
about the men who have fucked us before
and never returned for seconds, the veil
between worlds heavy as down comforters
and talk of dying fathers. I will float
through the wall, into the next apartment,
and hover like steaming breath in the room
over the sleeping family huddled
in one bed for warmth, desperate husband
separated by three squirming children
from safe harbor and helplessly erect,
the chill breeze on his skin—my phantom mouth.

John

The creak of the seesaw
in July darkness,
up, down, buzz-blond,
ice-blue eyes crinkling

with mirth at your own
anecdote—just home
from years in London,
tales of a bootshine

boy, of DJing,
photoshoots, drunk-dialing
Boy George at a party—
red, gold, and green,

we'd all shout—we're still
wet from the back lawn
of your parents' house,
trying to keep quiet,

only the soft rustle
of flesh on flesh
and the clicks and chirps
of nighttime creatures,

green stains on our elbows,
mud on our backs—
up, down, buzz-blond,
ice-blue eyes crinkling

at the corners,
something changes—we stop,
balanced perfectly
still, faces slack-jawed

in the silence, afraid
even to breathe,

as if we have both
noticed all at once

someone has noticed us
from a house nearby.
One of us whispers
I think we should go,

the barest groan
of the rust-hinged seesaw
marks our dismount,
panicked sprint together—

to the safe glow
of neighborhood streetlamps,
chests heaving, the held
breath rushing back out—

up, down, buzz-blond,
ice-blue eyes crinkling—
always just at the edge
of the circle of light,

and beyond it, sky,
indigo as old bruise—
my gut clenched in freefall,
this ride I can't get off.

Our First Time

Bare mattress lying on a clothestrewn floor,
the darkness like a third boy watching us
and touching himself, we lay still and scared,

breathing heavily, begin to fumble
and paw at our clothes thinking with one mind,
two heads what happens once we bare ourselves

and nothing is left between us, when we
have stuffed whatever we can of ourselves
into one another and then lay still.

Held tightly to the cleft of our bodies
in this attic, the party's bass thumping
from the floor below like an old woman

hitting her ceiling with a broom handle,
pot smoke seeping through the insulation,
I push my face fully into the nape

of your neck, your sweat or mine running down
over my nose and through the failing seal
of my pressed lips. I want only to breathe

us, what we have done, whatever we might
do next, but you—wide-eyed, confused, and new
to all of this—say nothing as you pull

your briefs—blue, I remember, with a green
band and light gray trim—back over your slim,
unvirgin buttocks and make for the stairs,

leaving me here covered in our cooling
wetness, alone with some family's packed-
away memories and settling dust.

Angel Trumpets, Devil Trombones:
A Stanley Kubrick Cento

I know it is madness to keep this journal, that it gives me
nothing but unorganized garbastic pieces so ugly
they could be a modern art masterpiece—mixture of tender,
dreamy childishness and a kind of eerie vulgarity.
Great merciful bloodstained gods, your pardon. Millions of years
of evolution, right? Reasonable, pleasant, phlegmatic—
I've been to a world's fair, a picnic, a rodeo, arms race,
peace race, space race. Places are like people—
some shine and some don't. Privately I believe in none of them.
Painters, nudists, writers, weightlifters—this republic of ours
is something like a rich widow. Weapon of iron and wood,
a big plane like a 52, bird of rarest-spun heaven
metal, exhaust frying chickens in the barnyard. Life goes on.
Always does until it doesn't. Men on the moon, men spinning,
gravity all nonsense. Can't be helped. Sorry about the mess.

Kevin

Sweet talking me over the Internet,
nights full of flirtation sent out across
six hours of daunting coastline from Boston
to small-town PA, its arbitrary
borders suddenly bars on a green cage.

But instead of coming to me, or me
to you, you have the novel idea
of our meeting in rural Kentucky—
having been nowhere, having done nothing,
I am rolling my new black Samsonite

through a terminal, my first sight of you
clutching a tan folder labeled *Secret
Date Itinerary. Not for Chad's Eyes!*
And I would have followed you anywhere.
Caving, my claustrophobia bricked up

in my chest, the warmth of your hand in mine
even as we squeeze through capillaries
in the earth's legs, following you deeper
down the Bourbon Trail, I a nondrinker
feigning interest in casks and sediment

when I'm really studying the small hairs
on the nape of your neck, and how little
it really takes to make them stand on end,
touring the glass factory, our faces
reflected and distorted everywhere—

fried everything at the local diner,
nothing compares to the taste of your skin
still on my tongue, like a ticket clutched tight
in my hands. I don't know where I'm going,
but I know this—home is where we return

when our travels are done, square-jawed marine

biologists who love the arts and fuck
like stallions, eyes every goddamned sunset
the world over, they just fly into my life
and fly out again, rhythmic as the tides

we hunt fossils in, by the waning light
of the day I fall for you, of the night
I let my guard down completely, heady
from Persian food, a local production
of *Raisin in the Sun*, and a long walk

to the moonlit hotel room, silhouettes
of swaying hemlock in the night wind's thrall—
helpless. I will never see you again.
Panicked on the flight home, sure I have left
something important in that hotel room,

eyes on the sun gleaming off winding streams,
quicksilver serpents, enticing, headless—
a child behind me is screaming, kicking.
We are swallowed by a glacial white cloud.
I left something there. You have taken it.

Microfiber Handkerchief

Left Pocket

For some reason I tap you, your face one
of many Brady Bunch squares competing
for attention—swirling backlit cauldron
of torso meat, eggplant, peach, arrows up
and down, conspicuously capital
Ts. And yet you ask *are you clean?* as if
did you mop the floor? in which case am I
the floor, or the mop, or the guileless hand
gripping it? And whatever I answer
won't satisfy you, the way fucking you
hard won't satisfy me, the way a smith
rains hammers on the shapes that rise unloved
from the steaming water. *Nothing is clean.*

Right Pocket

Desire in the quotidian, washing
dishes like technicolor drag Glinda,
bent over her iridescent bubble,
the high whine of vacuum and dog whimpers
to cover guttural grunts, gray dust puffs
jostled from the bag. There is an order
to everything, what keeps slipped-off shoes
in their cubbies, monogrammed his-and-his
hand towels draped on their racks, a cascade
of disparate throw pillows all arranged
perfectly. What is dirty in me craves
to be scrubbed, in the cycle of making,
unmaking—only this small disorder,
these domesticated beasts rattling chains.

Anthony

After you swallow
a fistful of pills

and call to tell me,
I don't have your name

to give the medics
who burst in the room—

I know what your coat
smells like in the rain

outside your building,
where the little shrimp

in your fish tank roams
when he scuttles by,

how your face scrunches
when you go to work

on my lower half—
They wheel you away,

maggot-pale, dark hair
slicked but for one strand

over your closed eyes,
talking to myself

in an empty hall,
I don't know. I don't—

how have I never
had to know your name?

Bryan

In shock, form loses
function; function, form.

Simple geometries
I've taken for granted—

the parabolic curve
of your bare ass

in curtained moonlight,
a conic bouquet

of just-because roses,
the oblate spheroid

we inhabit together
skews, warps, dissembles.

Instead, a great mass
of jumbled shapes—a closed

hotel door, *do not
disturb* circling the handle,

a steamed glass plane,
your hand, white against it,

the wide arc of soap
where it slid before finding

an angle to brace—
and the rest of you

and him against the tile
wall, the logistics

of how you fit together,
streaming hot water,

and the sound waves—moans,
the squeak of skin on glass,

the reedy hum your phone makes
on the edge of the sink,

each time I call and
call and get no answer.

Matthew

We're twenty, nude, everything firm
and responsive to the touch, soft
breeze cool on our flanks as the pool
laps small waves at the edges, night
purpling above us. You tell me

you have feelings, but I am young
enough to believe chemistry
waits dormant in all things for fire
to ignite—that perfect bonds form
on a whim. Years pass by in months,

six not talking, three back in touch,
each fuck-of-the-week with his flaws
you sob to me—the built frat boy
with awful car playlists, the twink
who texts you from across the room,

the circuit boy who makes the *clack-
clack* of credit cards on mirrors
every morning as he cuts
his breakfast lines. And each painting
you finish with a casual

mastery, sneaking some aspect
of one of them onto canvas—
the hyperreal Spartan soldier
who looks exactly like the guy
really into getting tied up,

the abstract square that is the house
you move into for a few months
with the one with the high-pitched voice
that drives you to drink and tell me
in some drab diner, like always,

that you wish we could have made it

work. A tentacle of cold cream
slowly wraps around my coffee
as I joke *At least you'd paint me,*
and the whole dark is strangled pale
again.

Screen Test: East of Eden

for Paul Newman and James Dean

How could anyone decide between them,
dark hair coiffed, their jaws like flipped chrome lighters,
James in his buttoned-down button up, small

tantalizing triangle of chest bared,
Paul in his starched white, bowtie taut, unlit
cigarette blithely tucked behind one ear?

Kiss me, James implores him, dimples pocking
the impossible angles of his cheeks.
Can't here, Paul replies automatically.

This isn't about who ends up as Cal,
dancing through bean fields in pared-down Steinbeck,
isn't about *did they* or *didn't they*,

because even though James will be crumpled
in his precious Porsche like tinfoil next year
and all the men who will toss Paul's salad

dressing in their carts sixty years later
won't care if his cool hands ever ran down
James's back, if Paul's lips ever tasted

the sweet bird of his youth, they're forever
flirting in the click and hiss of whirling
celluloid. But perhaps they'll meet again

offscreen, now that they've left the stage—somewhere
in a lush green garden, two men walking
hand in hand, uncovered and unashamed.

Nick

You are on my back and we
are running and singing
for a while just like
any two people in love
might do on a Spring day,

pretending to be
a cartoon plumber
astride a green dinosaur
humming their chiptune theme
on a campus sidewalk

before a truck rushes by,
hurls cruelties out the window
easy as a flicked cigarette
sparking on the road
like steel off flint,

or a used condom
like a stepped-on slug,
or a Gatorade bottle
filled with two hundred miles
of warm piss—

but it's none of these,
just a simple drive-by
with one word hitting us
like a Louisville slugger
off a tin mailbox. *Faggots.*

Tattered Handkerchief

Left Pocket

Means I'm into childhood trauma. Tell me
about the time you skinned your knee. Skin it
back and forth, hand cupping gingerly, big
wheel idling, alone. *Show me on the doll*
where they cut you, where the base of your pain
grows proud from its mound, desperate to root
anywhere else. I like to think that loss
is more than flesh wounds, more than the people
who scrape against our lives, each taking one
of our finite layers in their passing.
And we are docked more than a flap of skin
for this lesson, that what bares itself, red
and shining to the hungry open air
cannot ever be covered up again.

Right Pocket

I want to let you lie on top of me,
still as sediment, wait for the motion
of the earth grinding deep into itself;
or the earth spinning like a desk globe slapped
over and over by a bored schoolboy;
or the earth whipping around its orbit
like the same child beating a tetherball;
or the earth hurtling through the vast blackness
like that child flying, legs up, on his bike
over asphalt, at night, spurred by the thought
that the road continues unseen ahead—
and that shapes, resolving in their passing,
are unable to stop him from putting
his feet back on the pedals and pumping.

Brandon

Wide-eyed at nineteen with the world
      still wheeling on its axis unquestioned
            when you claim you can feel the full-

tilt lurch of the earth with each thrust
      of my hips—and dog-eared political
            texts piled on your bed are a poor

substitute for a boyfriend. How many
      times did we do this? How many
            more have taken my place inside you since?

Five years later, your picture dings
      on a sleazy sex app—*Young. Smart. Worldly.*
            your profile proclaims. *Now your turn.*

All those books you took as gospel and men
      you took in turn, never knowing
            that this, too, was a kind of politics.

I Fucked Your Ex-Boyfriend Last Night Because

I thought if I fucked the guy fucked over
by the guy who famously fucked me over,
I might get over it—but that's fucked up.

I fucked your ex-boyfriend last night because
it gave me closure—him closing around me—
and it seemed like the logical conclusion
to slurping pho in a dive restaurant
and awkward leg contact during HGTV.

I fucked your ex-boyfriend last night because
he has these black-rimmed hipster glasses,
and these short ginger curls in a low-top fade,
and his barking laugh startles a small room into silence,
and there was a pause in the conversation
we were desperate to fill with anything at all

that wasn't you.

Fun Fact: The Human Body is Three Hundred Ninety Percent Water

That long hair you always pluck from your cheek
and the pale fingers that pinch the tweezers

are water. Your raw, conflicted feelings
about your father's alcoholism

are water. That red line down your forearm
you insist is from startling your Maine Coon

in the middle of the night is water.
This poem is nothing more than water

flowing from the dark lagoon in the cleave
of my skull into yours, all the flotsam

from our lives comingling in the current,
all of it water. You pour a tall glass

from the curved spigot, watch as the bubbles
settle, then stop, wonder who this water

might have been—was he honest? Did he have
long hair? Did he insist that Elton John

song went *Hold me closer, Tony Danza,*
then think about how lovely that would be,

just your water swirled in his, murmuring
with wet lips, *You're the boss, you—No, you are.*

Andrew

Our first date with Slavoj Žižek,
a philosophy lecture, free

at the art museum, front row
in folding chairs sipping hot tea,

your idea of courtship. Charmed
by Žižek, deaf to everything

but the sound of his Slovene voice
slurring his words into thick stew,

shaggy grey face like a wire fox
terrier. *I say I love you,*

Žižek posits, pleased with himself,
only the way a poet does.

He says it again for effect.
Your eyes flash like slate blue diodes.

Later, you update your Facebook
with this quote as if it's brilliant.

Of course a poet knows nothing
of love. I didn't ride the train

here with a dog-eared book of Proust
for show. And you won't hear from me

that I love you in any way,
even though I scan your soft lips

for an opening while Žižek
mutters, rational and empty.

David

Like the statue, slender
alabaster, curly locks,

the soft, full face
of youth, sublime

in stillness, yet each muscle
prepared to move—

We meet in the throb
of sound, neon-strobe

over the curves of you,
fragmented light pocks

the crowded room—wordless,
we move closer.

In a vinyl alcove booth,
pretending we are VIPs,

we speak of mutual love
of Neil Gaiman, characters

printed and drawn, of Tori
Amos, her elemental voice—

soft lips moving those few
moments they are not busy

pressed to mine, young
and ravenous. You stand,

hands on your hips, the back
of your neck, contrapposto—

you tell me tomorrow
you'll be on a plane

home to Alaska, my arms
tight around you. *I had*

a northern lad. Well,
not exactly had...

We spill into yellow
sodium streetlight, wet July,

mutter quick promises,
and an idling cab steals you,

slinks into rain-blurred
Philadelphia—gone.

Perfectly Sensible Advice: A Jane Austen Cento

I have no notion of loving people by halves—I jump
from admiration to love, from love to matrimony.

Have as many holds upon happiness as possible.
Happiness in marriage is entirely a matter

of chance, for there will be little rubs and disappointments
everywhere, and pictures of perfection make me sick.

Let us have the luxury of silence, cold politeness.
When pain is over, remembrance of it often becomes

pleasure. Be composed, for what are men to rocks and mountains?
Dear gentlemen, I should infinitely prefer a book.

Conservative Handkerchief

Left Pocket

My legacy will stand, dark and glossy
like a finger sunk to the last knuckle
in your seat of power, a monument
to emoluments, lording over you
like a ziggurat, bastion of a bronzed
aged god—*look upon my works, ye mighty,
and depants.* Everything I am given
is my due, life grabbed unrepentantly
by the pussy, yowling and scrabbling claws
with my small hand on the scruff of its neck,
failing to comprehend the difference
between petting and strangling—all the while
whispering into its panic-flicked ear,
Shh, believe me, I know what I'm doing.

Right Pocket

I want your hands, fresh from signing a bill
to take away my healthcare, my access
to the pill that stops transmission of blood-
borne, slow cyanide, bubbling up your pen
onto my clean page, to bend me over
a desk of laws that thoroughly fuck me
over, so hard I have all the bloody,
cold calculus of it tattooed backwards
on my cheeks. Tell me I've been a naughty
little constituent, tell me I love
when you smack the marriage right out of me
and the fiscal responsibility
right in, so deep it feels ingrained, so hard
I want to pull a lever in your name.

Empty Parking Lot with You and Me and Ingmar Bergman

hot on your tongue, as if perfectly normal
to follow a first date's subpar bistro fare
and Woody Allen's latest with more
cinematic babble—*it's all been done before,*
you say, every screenplay a réchauffé
stewed in its own juices, adrift in orange-green
static of peas, carrots, cliché. Long after
I forget your name, the feel of your clammy hand
in mine, and the dark façade of the closed Whole Foods
we pass, where you walk slightly ahead
to dodge a puddle and I'm not checking out
organic produce in the window, I'll recall
Through a Glass Darkly, the way the August night's
silence says everything I want to hear.

Richard Pryor Slept with Marlon Brando, Pryor's Widow Confirms

Imagine them—Marlon, all sex and smooth-
bodied, claims a barstool, calls for Stella
Artois in its slim-necked and foam-shawled flute.
Dressed down between shoots, the white wife-beater
hugging broad swaths of long-labored muscle.

Richard is hunched three stools down, nursing gin,
his tawny lips wet with juniper tang,
the folded blue brim of a baseball cap
shading his face, drumming spindly fingers
on the polished bar, noting where they stick.

Marlon glides over with the easy grace
of predatory fish, and his rough hand
is on Richard's knee—bold, yet casual,
as if it has always been there, always
would be there. Perhaps there are words exchanged.

Perhaps some things transcend language—what moves
Richard from stiff-backed surprise to stumbling,
hand in hand, down a long hotel hallway
with Marlon's sandpapery chin brushing
the nape of his neck? It doesn't matter.

There are no celebrities in the dark—
only bodies, pushing, straining to fill
the emptiness inside one another
as long as they can, as long as the thin,
floral-papered walls keep the world at bay.

In the years to come, they will think of this—
mid-soliloquy, mid-pause for laughter,
mid-embrace with a woman they don't love—
if somewhere in the credits of their lives,
a name stands out, rising. Meaning something.

Leather Handkerchief

Left Pocket

Means I look for love in the wrong places—
the bottom of a bottle of poppers,
up an ass. I want shrill Doo-Wop to play
as we thud foreheads while craning our necks
to sip from the same man like one big straw
jutting from a malt glass. I want to say
how graceful you look in a sling, unzip
the black gimp mask like parting dawn's curtains
to kiss you sweetly for the first time, drop
you off in a parking lot, nude, covered
in Sharpie degradations to jog home
three miles, your house key duct taped to your leg
like after a first date, wondering how
it went, if you like me, who will call first.

Right Pocket

Below a buzzing neon TRUCK STOP sign,
its S burnt out, a haven for wayward
moths, I am tucked under the sweat-slick bulge
of your arm, exploring the dank, stubble-
studded mysteries thereunder, a pig
rooting truffles, drunk on his heady prize.
Maybe you have long hair; maybe your pate
is as smooth and reflective as mylar
in the balloons at your daughter's birthday;
maybe the freckles pocked on your cheek spell
love in Braille; maybe your smile is a string
of pearls resting on a tender pink throat.
What does it say about me—the last thing
I ever want in my mouth is your name?

Fun Fact: The Blood Vessels of a Blue Whale are Large Enough to Drive a 2018 Mitsubishi Outlander Sport Through

Just imagine getting lost in that whale,
wondering who else has been down this road
before, getting no cell signal, of course,

and not knowing how to read an atlas,
you pass a tow truck, its winched hook dangling
like a man's softness, nod to the driver

in that way men do sometimes, chin jutting
up, conceding nothing, as if to say
hello and *I could take you* all at once,

in the same motion. Then you will notice
the squareness of his shaven jaw, the way
his close-cropped blond hair makes his blue eyes pop,

and then he's there in your passenger seat,
you're off to find a dark capillary
to root in his lap like a truffle pig,

there in the rush of hot blood, leagues away
from anyone to judge you, his fingers
exploring up and down your seven inch

touch screen display, prone on the lush cloth seats,
deep in some poet's wine-dark Atlantic,
blue fleshy submarine pressing onward.

Rock and a Hard Place

for Rock Hudson

Can't be soft, but can't reveal what gets me
hard. All that heaven allows is to take

something polished and rough it up to hide
its luster, and when it cracks, hide that, too.

How eligible is a bachelor
when he's petrified? Lover, come back. Kiss

my granite cheek, my chiseled jaw. I'm here,
in the avalanche of pretty maids all

in a row, and you, my strange bedfellow,
have managed to crack me open. Inside,

I'm all jasper, carnelian, citrine,
malachite, lapis, amethyst—something

of value. Remember me as the man
in your arms, grinning in the sunstone glow

of your cigarette, sapphire eyes sparkling.
Forget the leading man they chipped from me,

the mined-out cavern I ended up. This
is my dynasty—written on the wind,

or a foreign name etched in my stone. Come
September, I'll be just another rock

buried in the earth. Don't visit me there.
Send me no flowers. Never say goodbye.

Walking in the Woods at Dusk to Lose Weight

Mine is not the sort of heart one hunts
in a forest. In the west, the color of clouds

boils down to the rheumy amber of cooked fat,
autumn's castoffs crunching like kettle chips

underfoot, the balls of my heels half-sucked
jawbreakers—prickled, drummed over the creek's

hard bones. I rest in dark fields, under the moon's
cragged nose, porous as seeded strawberries,

then home—its cold fountain of light, the evening's
serving of TV, the quiet phone, the cat.

Reading Myself to Sleep

I want to fall asleep with two great men
pressed on top of me, the weight of their years

leather-bound on my chest. I think of them—
Oscar, sandy hair swooped over one side

of his forehead like a volumized wave,
and Walt, all greyswept and windkissed tangles,

waistcoat full of crumbs. There is room for both
in me, what satisfies the soul rarely

pure, never simple. Three generations
of men and poems, no apologies.

I steeple the fingers of my left hand
with Oscar's—warm, soft, and damp—and my right

with Walt's—lifestudded, inkstained, cold as breeze-
blessed shale. They are the only men who stay.

GOLDEN | SHOVEL for ALAN | TURING

Remove the satisfaction and the act becomes hollow.
*—Alan **Turing***

crack the code MAN | MACHINE the world **believes**
is simple WRONG | RIGHT that like **machines**
men flip a switch OFF | ON and love they **think**

is an ENIGMA | SOLVED neatly **Turing**
tests the question FALSE | TRUE *are you alive?* **lies**
my DISGRACE | LEGACY time spent **with men**

| |

the lines PRIVATE | PUBLIC blurred and **therefore**
the conflict WAR | VICTORY muddles **machines**
will FORGET | REMEMBER me **do not think**

you CONDEMN | COMMEND me the fault's not **yours**
my rewards NEEDLE | MEDAL **in distress**
failed as Turing NUMB | NUMB now just **Alan**

Two for Tea

Without asking, the teahouse seats the two of us
in this season's theme room: *Homegrown Heroes,*

where the walls, instead of the usual white
grandmother parlor decor—lace, dainty, dated—

are a riot of redwhiteblue streamers likely bought
on July Fifth clearance at Party City,

and a jumble of cop and fireman paraphernalia
collected from over the years. Dinged helmets,

rusty badges, a length of dirty hose, chipped nightsticks
and old billy clubs dangle over us like doom

over Damocles. *How many of my people's brains,*
my friend asks, gesturing with a wide, dark finger

barely able to squeeze through the dainty cup's handle,
do you think those things bashed in? The air's all oolong,

subtle notes of sunsweet blueberry and tension.
Look at the knees on that Navy uniform,

I reply, a bite of sausage quiche balanced on my fork.
Don't they look a little worn out? We have dressed

in our Friday best—the platonic pair of gay white man
and straight (enough) Black married father of two.

The waitress, who is probably also the owner,
feigns a smile, but the *tsssks* that keep drifting our way

aren't the clinks of china on saucers or the hiss
of Earl Grey poured from a spout. The neighboring women

are whispering conspiratorially and glancing
furtively when they aren't busy stuffing themselves

with petit fours. I finish my rooibos, dab my lips
three times with a flourish of white napkin, then turn to them.

Hey, I ask, *what did the gay stag say after leaving
the tea house?* I wait a beat. They gape in surprise and fear.

Man, I finish, as we drop cash on the table
and rise to leave, *I blew like fifty bucks in there.*

Lilac Wine: A Nina Simone Cento

Sweet and heady, like my love. I tell ya—
this is a show tune, but the show hasn't
been written for it yet. I oughtta drink.

I left a note on his dresser with these
few goodbye words: *You ain't never been blue,
no. I'm ready, darling. Don't smoke in bed.*

I'm leaving my wedding ring. Unsteady.
It's gonna be like dying when he calls.
Don't let him handle me with his hot hands.

With a brick in my handbag and a smile
on my face, meeting is pleasure, parting
is pain, slow and steady, down to my shoes.

Men cluster to me like moths. All I have
are my arms to enfold you—so break down,
let it out, already. Wild is the wind.

Hadrian Addresses Marble Bust of Antinous

One who drinks from the Nile must return.
—Egyptian Proverb

History has deemed it an accident.
Would it help if I said I was sorry?
You're supposed to take lovers, they told me.

Not to fall in love. When we are afraid
of being remembered as soft, hard men
turn to stone. Each morning, I turn to stone

and weep over your face on the pillow
beside me, marblequiet. You are soft
where I am hard, warleathered hands squeezing

your buttersilk neck beneath the water—
wide-eyed, betrayed, until the bubbles stop.
I carry your face to the water's edge

again and again to kiss you goodnight
by moonlight, milksilver in the river.
But Nile is no Lethe. I can't forget

what I've done. I scoop a fistful of clay
from the riverbed, weep as the current
first softens it, then carries it away.

Alex

When will you write the poem about me?
you ask, driving to the aquarium.
I don't know. The sun, chiaroscuro

through dead Camden trees, strobes the fogged windows
of your car. You sing to me as you drive,
rich tenor thrumming Romantic poems

set to song. I am already planning,
midway through this gift, how best to explain
the conversational tone of the words

is lost to the music. As your voice ebbs
out, I tell you, *The conversational
tone of the words is lost to the music.*

In the gift shop, the glass-eyed turtleweights
and all manner of snap-jawed heads on sticks
are pawed by ravenous, juice-faced children.

Framed, paint-footed penguin paintings wander
the footpath between caprice and desire.
We have seen the hippo, joked about shit

tail-propelled, flung in a staccato cone
out of the enclosure. Our fingertips
graze in the long shark tunnel when the waves

of children pass. We cannot expose them
to terrifying aspects of nature
like same-sex love and expect them to cope.

I press against you in the dark corner
while a bassoon-bodied fish with pursed lips
watches from the other side of the glass.

My lips are dried from a cheap soft pretzel
and an entire afternoon of waiting
to tell you how I feel. Blue-hued caustics

cast ripples on your face as a stingray
glide-flaps by—your favorite. Childlike joy
flows over you. Over me watching you.

Your poem comes at the end, when the fish
have finished nipping and all darted off.
Whatever's left—this buoyant heart—is yours.

Acknowledgements

"Dear Mark Doty," "Christopher," "Invisible Handkerchief," "John," "Tattered Handkerchief," "Conservative Handkerchief," and "Richard Pryor Slept with Marlon Brando, Pryor's Widow Confirms" were performed on the radio show, "The Poet and the Poem" with Grace Cavalieri from the Library of Congress in March 2017, archived at the Library of Congress and on iTunes.

"Christopher," "Jesse," "Our First Time," "Brandon," "Fun Fact: The Human Body is Three Hundred Ninety Percent Water," "Lilac Wine: A Nina Simone Cento," and "Alex" were published in *Schuylkill Valley Journal,* Fall 2020.

"Andrea" and "Perfectly Sensible Advice: A Jane Austen Cento" were published in *Rag Queen Periodical,* June 2017.

"Dungeons &" and "Shepard" were published in ONE ART: *A Journal of Poetry* in July 2021. "Shepard" was nominated for a Pushcart Prize in 2021.

"Bruce" was published in *Philadelphia Stories* in 2019 as an Honorable Mention for the Sandy Crimmins National Prize in Poetry.

"Invisible Handkerchief," "Tattered Handkerchief," and "Conservative Handkerchief" were published in *Menacing Hedge* in Fall 2020. "Tattered Handkerchief" was nominated for Best of the Net in 2021.

"John" was published in *Wicked Gay Ways* in Summer 2020.

"Matthew" was published in *Philadelphia Stories* in 2020 as an Honorable Mention for the Sandy Crimmins National Prize in Poetry.

"Nick," "Andrew," and "David" were published in *Chantarelle's Notebook* in June 2020.

"Bryan" was published in *Indigent Press a La Carte* in Fall 2017.

"I Fucked Your Ex-Boyfriend Last Night Because" was published in *Philosophical Idiot* in July 2017.

"Nine-Year-Old Suicide in Reverse" was published in *Philadelphia Stories* in

2019 as a Runner Up for the Sandy Crimmins National Prize in Poetry.

"Empty Parking Lot with You and Me and Ingmar Bergman" was published on the Montgomery County Poet Laureate website montcopoet.org in January 2020 as part of an interview with Cathleen Cohen.

"Leather Handkerchief" was published in the *2018 Featured Poets Anthology* from Moonstone Press.

"Reading Myself to Sleep" was published under the previous title "Literary Handkerchief" in *Scripta* in April 2019.

Chad Frame's work appears in *Rattle, Pedestal, Barrelhouse, Rust+Moth, Philadelphia Stories, Menacing Hedge, River Heron Review*, and elsewhere, including on iTunes from the Library of Congress. He is the Director of the Montgomery County Poet Laureate Program and Poet Laureate Emeritus of Montgomery County, Pennsylvania, the Poetry Editor of *Ovunque Siamo*, a founding member of the No River Twice poetry improv performance troupe, and Founder and Director of the Caesura Poetry Festival and Retreat. He also writes fiction and screenplays, and loves cats, fencing, rolling polyhedral dice, lyrics-driven female singer-songwriters on piano, translating Latin, and you, too—whoever you are.